Victoi
Plant

CW01639049

Purnell

ISBN 0 361 05342 8

Published 1982 by Purnell Books, Paulton, Bristol BS18 5LQ
Made and printed in Great Britain by Purnell and Sons (Book Production) Limited, Paulton, Bristol

Summer in the Great Wood was a time when all the plants sent out extra bright green leaves in all directions. The grass grew thick and high all around Victoria Plum's house.

"Oh dear me," sighed Victoria as she struggled through it. "What a job it is to get to my front door! I shall have to cut all this grass down."

VP

As she did not have a lawn mower of her own, she borrowed one from the badger family who lived nearby. Soon there was a smooth, velvety lawn all around Victoria's front door.

"This is much better," thought Victoria as she paused for breath after mowing it. "The lawn looks neat and tidy now, as if someone really does care about it."

Mr. Badger poked his head out of the entrance to his home.

"Finished with the mower, have you?" he said. "Be making a nice little garden for yourself now, I suppose!"

“Well . . . it’s an idea,” said Victoria, thoughtfully. “A few flowers would look nice. Red ones . . . or yellow . . . or blue. There are so many colours I really don’t know which ones to choose.”

"Why not have them all?" said Mr. Badger. "You'll enjoy having a colourful garden." And he disappeared underground again.

Victoria went indoors and buttered herself an oat scone for tea, and then washed it down with a glass of blackberry juice. All through tea she was thinking about her garden.

Although she wasn't a senior fairy by any means, she knew enough magic to make herself a garden. She had only to go out, whisper a few magic words and borders would be dug and plants would flower in them in seconds.

"But our teacher always says that magic should only be used when there is no other way," she said to herself. "So really I should go out there and dig up the soil by myself, choose the plants and sow seeds myself."

Victoria was a good fairy and would never do what she knew to be wrong, so she decided to make her garden without using magic. Mr. Badger lent her his spade and she worked hard all evening before the sun went down, digging a wide, circular border several feet out from her tree.

"This is hard work," she said to herself. "I wish that Ben could be here to help me."

As she thought this, she saw a flash of somebody dressed in green in the wood beyond her.

"Ben!" she called. "Come and help."

Benjamin the elf was not too keen to start gardening just as dusk was falling in the wood. He had been playing Catch-Me-If-You-Can with the grey squirrels and was on his way home for a rest and a slice of cake.

But he was kind at heart and could not ignore Victoria's plea. Soon he was digging away, and Victoria was raking over the earth to smooth it, ready to plant her flowers.

"I'll have primroses, and bluebells, and lilies of the valley, and honeysuckle by the door," she said, happily. "Won't it look pretty, Ben?"

"I suppose I'll have to watch where I'm putting my feet," said Ben, crossly. He was still wishing he could be at home, eating his cake.

"Oh, you wouldn't want to tread on the plants, would you, Ben?" said Victoria, shocked.

"Well, no," admitted Ben. "We'll go looking for some pretty plants tomorrow, shall we?"

"What a good idea," said Victoria. "Let's stop now. Would you like a piece of my home-made cake, before you go home?"

Next day Victoria and Ben took a little basket and a trowel, and went about the wood collecting primrose plants. They were very careful to take only a few here and there to thin out a group which had become overcrowded, so that they would not be missed.

They brought the plants back and put them into the ground, and Victoria filled her teapot with water and gave them all a drink to settle them in.

"I haven't got a watering can," she said. "But I'm sure this teapot will do just as well."

Now it so happened that the very next day she got called away to visit an aunt who was not very well, and when she arrived home again she was dismayed to see that her garden was looking very sorry for itself. The grass was long again, and as for her primrose plants—well! There was hardly a leaf left on any of them, and what there was looked frayed and chewed. Victoria was quite horrified.

VP

"Whatever has happened?" she cried, dropping her suitcase on the ground and rushing over to look more closely.

There seemed to be no explanation for it—until Victoria noticed the silver thread of a slug between two of the tattered plants.

"You horrid slug!" she cried. "Eating all my plants! Ruining my garden!" She sat down on the grass and sobbed.

Presently she became aware that she wasn't the only one sobbing, and looking around her she saw that four of the naughty slugs had come out of hiding and were weeping quite noisily next to her. Victoria had never seen a weeping slug before so she stopped crying and looked at them in surprise.

"Nobody loves a slug!" cried the largest of the four. "Nobody welcomes us! We've got to eat, haven't we? And it was such a lovely smooth piece of ground to sit on while we chewed. And it wasn't just us, Victoria—the birds pecked the seeds that you planted for next year."

Victoria gazed upwards to the branches above her, and all the birds fell silent to prove that it was true.

"I'm very disappointed in all of you," she said, and went indoors.

Next day, when Ben and Victoria met for lessons, Victoria was still upset.

"How could you let them do it, Ben?" she asked. "You knew how much that garden meant to me."

"I'm sorry, Victoria," said Ben. "I didn't think."

The teacher, who had been writing something on the blackboard, turned round and looked at Victoria over the top of his spectacles.

"As you are more interested in gardening that magic this morning, I shall change the subject," he said. "We will learn about gardening."

He rubbed the board clean.

"Now," he said turning back to Victoria. "A garden should be a restful place. There should be something for everyone in it. Flowers, and smells, and food too, if necessary."

"But I don't want my flowers to be food!" cried Victoria. "I just want them to look pretty."

"Then you must provide other food," said the teacher. "Did you think, when you planted your garden, of the ground cover you were destroying? Or of all the food sources you were digging up?"

Victoria hung her head.

"No," she said, feeling rather ashamed.

"It was home for all the other creatures before it was your garden," said the teacher. "And you mustn't blame the birds for taking food where they find it."

"I'm sorry," said Victoria.
"Come," said the teacher. "We will put things right with a little magic."

There was much twittering and tapping out of messages that morning in the Great Wood. "Come to Victoria's garden", was the message passed from the bees to the butterflies, from the birds to the snails, from the slugs to the baby frogs who hopped up from the nearby river.

When they got there, what a change!

By magic, the garden was now full of glorious plants and food for everyone. There was a buddleia for the butterflies and cabbages for the slugs; tall sunflowers full of seeds for the birds and snapdragons for the bees. There was grass for tunnelling moles, a shady, wet patch for all the frogs and lots of flowers for Ben and Victoria.

"You know, I could get to like gardening," said Ben as he and Victoria sat on the lawn sipping mint tea. "Especially the magic kind!"